STAR WARS

FINN'S MISSION

Written by David Fentiman

Written and Edited by David Fentiman
Project Art Editor Owen Bennett
Pre-Production Producer Marc Staples
Senior Producer Alex Bell
Managing Editor Sadie Smith
Managing Art Editor Ron Stobbart
Art Director Lisa Lanzarini
Publisher Julie Ferris
Publishing Director Simon Beecroft

For Lucasfilm
Editorial Assistant Samantha Holland
Executive Editor Jonathan W. Rinzler
Image Archives Stacey Leong
Art Director Troy Alders
Story Group Leland Chee, Pablo Hidalgo, and Rayne Roberts

First American Edition, 2016
Published in the United States by DK Publishing
345 Hudson Street, New York, New York 10014

Page design copyright © 2016 Dorling Kindersley Limited
DK, a Division of Penguin Random House LLC
16 17 18 19 20 10 9 8 7 6 5 4 3 2 1
001–280674–June/2016

© & TM 2016 LUCASFILM LTD.

A catalog record for this book is available from the Library of Congress.

ISBN 978-1-4654-5131-6 (Hardback)
ISBN 978-1-4654-5101-9 (Paperback)

DK books are available at special discounts when purchased in bulk for sales promotions,
premiums, fund-raising, or educational use. For details, contact: DK Publishing Special
Markets, 345 Hudson Street, New York, New York 10014
SpecialSales@dk.com

Printed and bound in China

A WORLD OF IDEAS:
SEE ALL THERE IS TO KNOW

www.dk.com
www.starwars.com

Contents

4 Stormtroopers
6 Stormtrooper equipment
8 The planet Jakku
10 Stormtrooper training
12 Battle at the village
14 Running away
16 First Order vehicles
18 Crash!
20 Finn in the desert
22 Jakku animals
24 Niima Outpost
26 Rey and Finn
28 BB-8
30 Escape from Jakku
32 Dogfight over the desert
34 Han and Chewie
36 Rathtars
38 Trouble with gangsters
40 Maz
42 Maz's castle
44 Castle crooks
46 Battle at the castle
48 General Leia Organa
50 Finn's mission
52 Attacking the Starkiller
54 Getting inside
56 Mission accomplished
58 Quiz
60 Glossary
62 Guide for Parents

64 Index

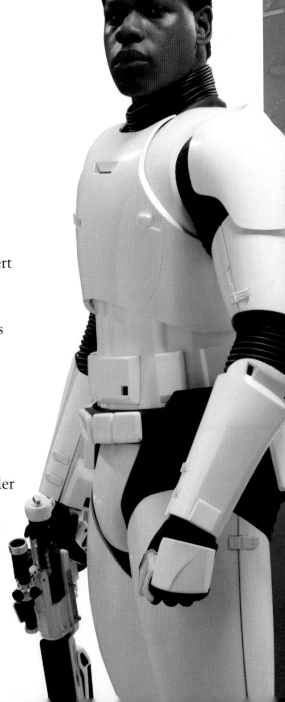

Stormtroopers

Many years ago, the evil Galactic Empire ruled the galaxy. The Empire's soldiers wore shining white armor and were feared for their cruelty. These soldiers were known as stormtroopers.

Eventually the people of the galaxy rebelled and fought back, and the Empire was destroyed.

The survivors of the Empire have spent years planning their revenge. They have renamed themselves the First Order. Now a new generation of stormtroopers is preparing to conquer the galaxy. One of these troopers is known as FN-2187.

> STORMTROOPER EQUIPMENT

HELMET:

> Made out of strong betaplast

> Contains communications gear and a head-up display to assist with targeting

ARMOR:

> Built to deflect or soften hits from blasters or physical impacts

> It is tough but very light

FLAMETHROWER:

> The D-93 incinerator fires a powerful jet of burning gel that ignites anything it touches

> It is a very dangerous and unpredictable weapon

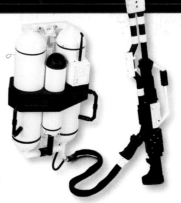

MEGABLASTER:

> The FWMB-10 megablaster is a heavy weapon designed for use against armored targets

> It has an extendable support to allow accurate firing

RIOT BATON:

> The Z6 riot-control baton is used to control crowds on worlds ruled by the First Order

> Its electrical shock vanes can give someone a powerful jolt

BLASTER RIFLE:

> The F-11D blaster rifle is a stormtrooper's primary weapon

> It is designed to be tough, accurate, easily adaptable, and simple to use

The planet Jakku

Jakku is a hot, dry, and dusty planet. It was the site of a terrible battle between the Empire and the Rebel Alliance. Thousands of starships fought each other above the planet, and many of them crashed to the ground.

Years after the battle, there are groups of scavengers on Jakku who make a living taking scrap from the old starship wrecks.

In the Kelvin Ravine, a small group of religious worshippers has built a village. The villagers do not realize that they have something the First Order wants very badly, and an army of stormtroopers is coming to take it.

STORMTROOPER TRAINING

The First Order uses advanced simulations to train its stormtroopers. These practice runs test them for agility, endurance, coordination, and accuracy. The stormtroopers are being trained to battle a group known as the Resistance, which has been fighting against the First Order's forces.

FN-2187 SCORECARD

AGILITY TEST:
Ability to complete
an obstacle course
Score: **8/10**

ENDURANCE TEST:
Ability to run 10
kilometers while
wearing armor
Score: **9/10**

**COORDINATION
TEST:**
Ability to perform
multiple tasks at once
Score: **8/10**

ACCURACY TEST:
Ability to hit a moving
target with a blaster
Score: **9/10**

Well done, FN-2187.
You have been ranked
as ready for combat
operations. Please submit
your scores to the training
sergeant for processing.

Battle at the village

FN-2187's first battle is on Jakku. He and his fellow stormtroopers are sent to attack the village in the Kelvin Ravine. The villagers fight back, and FN-2187 is shocked when one of his friends, FN-2003, gets hit. FN-2187 spends the rest of the battle in a daze.

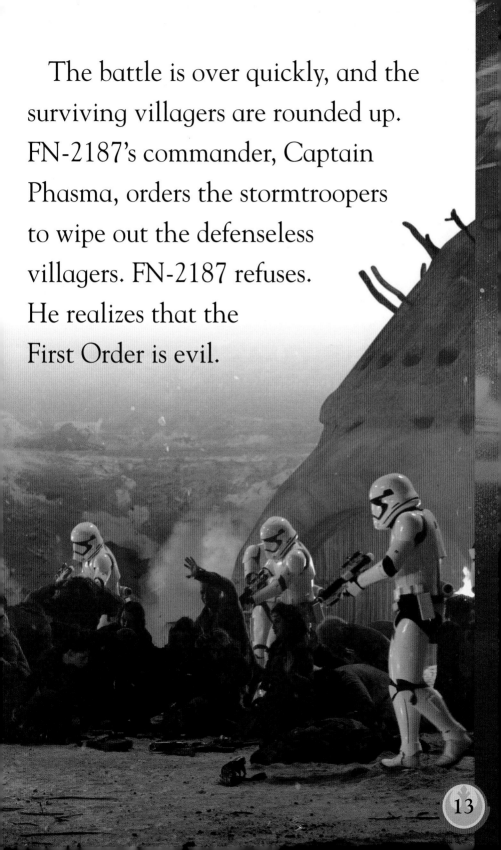

The battle is over quickly, and the surviving villagers are rounded up. FN-2187's commander, Captain Phasma, orders the stormtroopers to wipe out the defenseless villagers. FN-2187 refuses. He realizes that the First Order is evil.

Running away

FN-2187 wants to escape from the First Order, but he is trapped. He is stuck on board a Star Destroyer and he does not have a ship to escape on, or know how to fly one.

FN-2187 has an idea. The First Order has captured a pilot from the Resistance. If FN-2187 can release him, they can steal a ship together and escape.

The pilot is named Poe Dameron. FN-2187 rescues him from his cell and they rush to the hangar. They jump into a TIE fighter and fly away from the Star Destroyer. Poe asks FN-2187 what his name is. When he tells him, Poe says he should change it to "Finn."

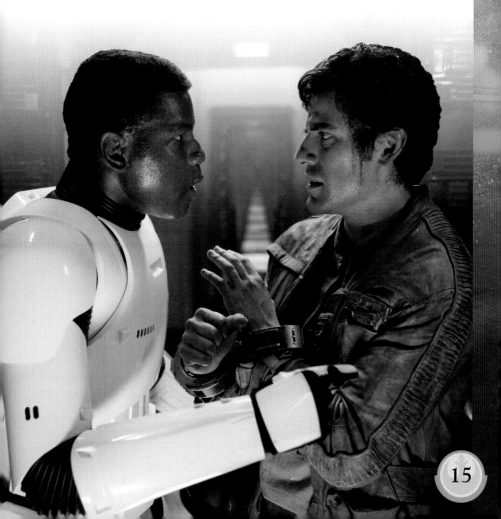

FIRST ORDER VEHICLES

The First Order has many powerful war machines. These vehicles all perform different tasks.

TROOP TRANSPORTER

Troop transporters carry stormtroopers from their base or Star Destroyer into battle. They can unload up to 20 stormtroopers at a time.

STAR DESTROYER

Star Destroyers are huge ships. They are thousands of meters long and carry crews that number in the tens of thousands. A single Star Destroyer can use its TIE fighters and stormtroopers to conquer an entire planet.

COMMAND SHUTTLE

Command shuttles are used
to carry important people
from one place to another.
Generals, admirals, or other
high-ranking officials each
have their own shuttle.

TIE FIGHTER

TIE fighters are the First
Order's main attack craft.
They are fast and agile,
and their laser cannons
can destroy other ships
or targets on the ground.

Crash!

Finn and Poe shoot at the Star Destroyer as they escape in their TIE fighter. They cause a lot of damage, but before they can get away, the Star Destroyer fires back.

Their ship is hit, and it begins to spiral down toward Jakku. Finn manages to eject, and he parachutes into the desert.

After he lands, Finn rushes to the crash site. He can't find Poe, but he discovers Poe's jacket in the wreckage. Finn takes his stormtrooper armor off and puts the jacket on to disguise himself. He looks around, but he can't see anyone nearby.

Finn in the desert

Finn is alone in the desert. Without water he won't last very long in such a hot, dry place. The area he is in is known as the Sinking Fields. There is dangerous quicksand that will suck him down if he is not careful.

After hours walking through the desert, Finn finally arrives at a town. It is called Niima Outpost.

Finn is desperate for a drink.
He finds a water trough, but he has
to share it with a giant stinking
creature known as a happabore!

Jakku Animals

Jakku has some very strange animal species. The locals find uses for most of them, but some are dangerous and are best avoided.

Steelpecker

Diet: metal, usually in the form of junk

Uses: Steelpecker droppings contain valuable elements

Nightwatcher worm

Diet: carnivorous

Uses: none (highly dangerous)

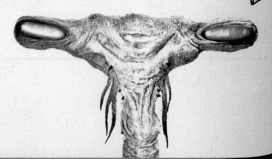

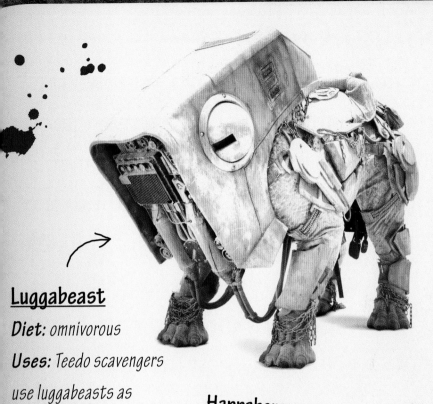

Luggabeast

Diet: *omnivorous*

Uses: *Teedo scavengers use luggabeasts as pack animals*

Happabore

Diet: *omnivorous*

Uses: *can be used to pull heavy loads, or ridden as transportation*

Niima Outpost

Niima Outpost is the biggest town on Jakku. It is the center of the scavenging industry that has formed on the planet. From here, scavengers travel out into the Starship Graveyard to search for valuable technology inside the huge wrecks.

When they find something, they bring it back to Niima Outpost to trade. They don't get paid with money, though. Instead, the junk dealers give them food rations.

It is a hard life being a scavenger. Exploring the rusting wrecks of old starships is very dangerous. There are also bands of thieves in the desert that might rob them, and dangerous creatures that could eat them.

Rey and Finn

Finn is worried that the First Order might be searching for him. He is trying to hide at Niima Outpost when he sees a girl and a droid being attacked by some thugs. The girl defeats them, but then she sees Finn, and she comes running up to him.

She knocks Finn down but then
she stops. She has seen Poe's jacket
and thinks that Finn must be a
member of the Resistance. As the
stormtroopers come after them,
she grabs Finn's hand and they
escape together. Her name is Rey.

BB-8

BB-8 is a Resistance astromech droid. It turns out he used to belong to Poe Dameron, but he was left behind when Poe got captured. Rey found BB-8 out in the desert, and she brought him to Niima Outpost.

Articulated holoprojector array

Power recharge port

Cooling vents

Primary
photoreceptor

High
frequency
receiver
antenna

Escape from Jakku

Finn, Rey, and BB-8 need to leave Jakku. The First Order is chasing them and they need to find a ship to escape on, quickly! The first ship they look at is known as a quadjumper. It has four huge engines and looks fast, but before Finn can climb on board, TIE fighters swoop in and destroy it.

The next ship is underneath
a tarpaulin. They run over and
climb inside. The ship looks old
and battered, but they start the
engines and take off. Finn does
not know it, but this is one of the
most famous ships in the galaxy.
It is the *Millennium Falcon*.

Dogfight over the desert

Finn and Rey are in trouble!
The *Millennium Falcon* is being chased
by First Order TIE fighters. Unless
they can think of a way to escape,
they will get shot down for sure!

Finn jumps into the gun turret of the
Millennium Falcon.
From here he can
try to shoot down
the ships that are
chasing them.
It's hard to aim,
but Finn's
stormtrooper
training means he
is a good shot.

Rey decides to fly the *Millennium Falcon* inside an old wrecked starship. Only the bravest or most foolish First Order pilots will follow them through here.

After a hectic chase, the *Millennium Falcon* is able to get away!

Han and Chewie

Finn and his new friends have escaped from Jakku, but their problems are only just beginning. The *Millennium Falcon* breaks down, leaving them stranded in space.

Finn and Rey try to repair it, but a giant star freighter appears and swallows the *Millennium Falcon* whole!

The ship that swallows the *Millennium Falcon* belongs to Han Solo and Chewbacca, two of the most famous heroes in the galaxy.

Han and Chewie used to own the *Millennium Falcon*. They are surprised to find Finn and Rey on their old ship, but they agree to help them. It turns out Han is transporting some animals on his freighter for a wealthy client. The creatures are known as rathtars.

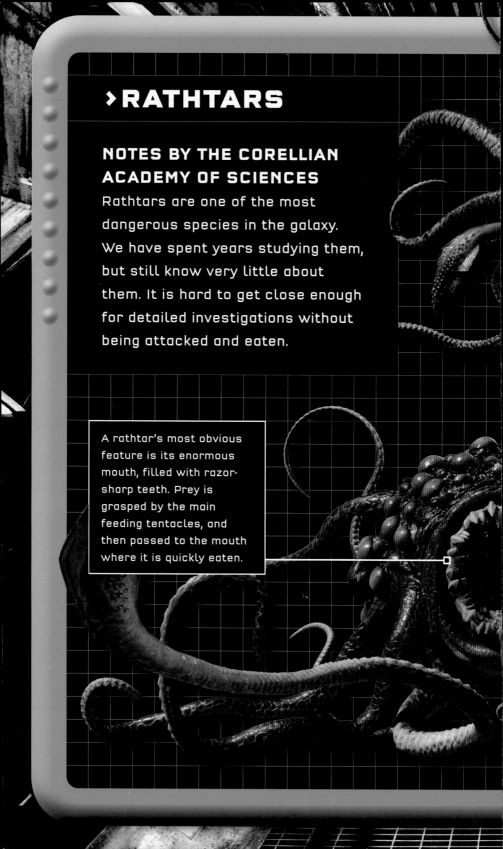

›RATHTARS

NOTES BY THE CORELLIAN ACADEMY OF SCIENCES

Rathtars are one of the most dangerous species in the galaxy. We have spent years studying them, but still know very little about them. It is hard to get close enough for detailed investigations without being attacked and eaten.

A rathtar's most obvious feature is its enormous mouth, filled with razor-sharp teeth. Prey is grasped by the main feeding tentacles, and then passed to the mouth where it is quickly eaten.

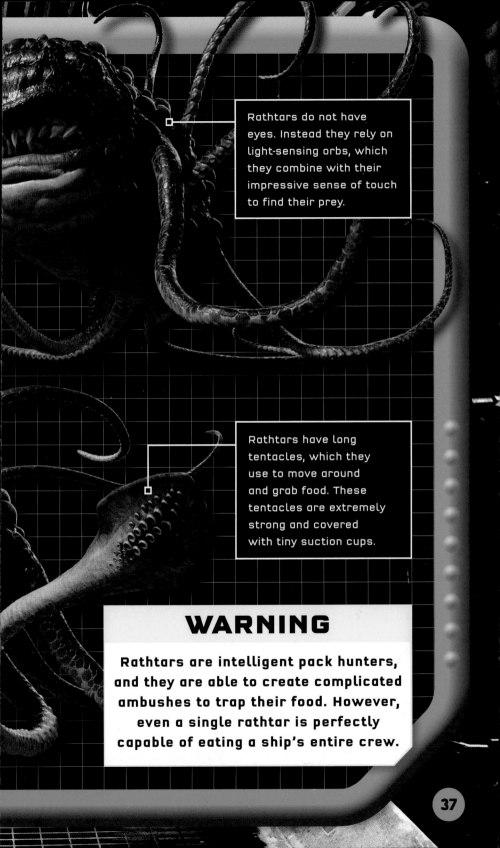

Rathtars do not have eyes. Instead they rely on light-sensing orbs, which they combine with their impressive sense of touch to find their prey.

Rathtars have long tentacles, which they use to move around and grab food. These tentacles are extremely strong and covered with tiny suction cups.

WARNING

Rathtars are intelligent pack hunters, and they are able to create complicated ambushes to trap their food. However, even a single rathtar is perfectly capable of eating a ship's entire crew.

Trouble with gangsters

Han and Chewie have made a lot of enemies over the years. They have done business with some very dangerous criminals and have not always kept their word.

Two gangs have come looking for Han and Chewie. The first is the scruffy Kanjiklub, led by Tasu Leech. The second is the scary Guavian Death Gang, led by Bala-Tik.

Both gangs board Han's freighter and confront him. Suddenly, the rathtars get loose. There is chaos as the monsters start eating the gang members. Finn and his friends all rush on board the *Millennium Falcon* and escape.

Maz Kanata

Han wants to get help from an old friend of his. He flies the *Falcon* to an ancient castle on the planet Takodana. This is the home of Maz Kanata, one of the most famous pirates in the galaxy.

Maz has known Han and Chewie for decades. She helped Han when he first started out as a smuggler. She may be small, but she makes up for it with her big personality, and her ability to use the Force.

The Force is a strange energy. It allows those who can sense it to perform incredible feats, like reading other people's minds. When the Jedi Order still existed, the Jedi used the Force to protect the weak and defend justice.

MAZ'S CASTLE

Welcome to Maz's castle, one of the most exciting places in the galaxy! If you're new here, there are a few rules you need to follow:

1. No fighting. Maz will not accept violence under her roof. Anyone caught fighting will be removed from the castle and may be punished.

2. No politics. It doesn't matter which group, planet, or faction you belong to. Wars and diplomacy are left outside, and no one gets special treatment.

3. Do not cheat. There are all kinds of games to play in the castle, including dejarik and sabacc. Have fun, but don't be tempted to cheat or you'll find yourself in big, big trouble.

4. Do not steal. There are a lot of ancient artifacts in the castle. Some of them are dangerous. Don't be tempted to take anything or it could be the last thing you do!

Castle crooks

Maz's castle is popular with some of the roughest criminals in the galaxy. There are smugglers, pirates, thieves, bounty hunters, and assassins all under one roof.

Normally, having so many violent lawbreakers in one place would be a disaster. Luckily, they all follow Maz's rules and so fights are rare. Instead, the guests compete with each other using games like sabacc, dejarik, and droid fighting.

One of the meanest of them all is Grummgar. This huge creature is a hunter and mercenary who enjoys poaching rare animals. The other guests avoid him. They know he could easily smash them to pieces!

Battle at the Castle

The First Order has a spy in Maz's Castle, and now knows that Finn and his friends are there. An army of stormtroopers lands to capture Finn and take him back to be punished.

Maz gives Finn an old lightsaber so he can defend himself. He joins Han and Chewie to fight back. There is a ferocious battle, and although Finn fights bravely he is outnumbered and has to surrender.

Suddenly the Resistance arrive.
It's Poe! He survived the crash
on Jakku and he has brought the
other Resistance pilots with him.
The First Order forces retreat, but
Rey is captured and taken away.

General Leia Organa

Finn, Han, Chewie, and BB-8 travel to the Resistance base on the planet D'Qar. The base is buried underground, and Finn is surprised by how old and overgrown it is. At the base they talk with the Resistance's leader, General Leia Organa.

Leia is respected by everybody in the Resistance.

Her part in the rebellion against the Empire is legendary. They know that she will lead them to victory over the First Order.

Many in the Resistance don't trust Finn. They know he was once a stormtrooper and they worry that he might betray them. Leia, though, does trust Finn. She can sense the courage inside him, and she knows Finn has a vital role to play in the battle to come.

FINN'S MISSION

YOU HAVE VOLUNTEERED TO ATTACK THE FIRST ORDER'S STARKILLER WEAPON.

Here is what we currently know about this weapon:

• It is based on an unnamed ice planet. The temperatures are extremely cold, and you will need to be prepared for snowy conditions.

• It has the ability to destroy an entire star system. A short while ago the weapon was used against the New Republic capital on Hosnian Prime. Reports are still coming in, but we believe the whole system has been devastated.

• It is guarded by legions of stormtroopers, squadrons of TIE fighters, missile batteries, and turbolaser turrets.

• It is defended by a nearly impenetrable deflector shield. This will have to be deactivated if the Starkiller is going to be attacked from above.

• Its only point of weakness is its thermal oscillator. This is your target. If it is destroyed, the Starkiller will tear itself apart.

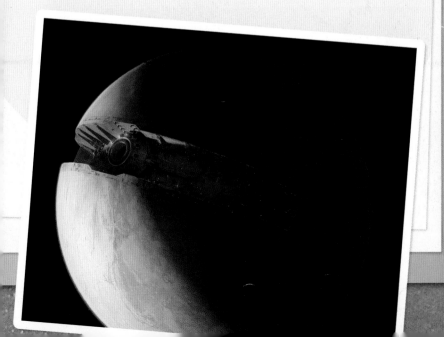

Attacking the Starkiller

Finn's mission is very dangerous. Finn, Han, and Chewie use the *Millennium Falcon*'s hyperdrive to pass through the Starkiller's deflector shield, and land on the Starkiller planet.

They manage to sneak inside the base and turn off the Starkiller's deflector shield. Now the brave Resistance pilots can attack the thermal oscillator.

Finn doesn't know it, but Rey has escaped from her cell. They run into each other, but quickly they realize that there is a problem. The Resistance pilots can't shoot through the thermal oscillator's thick armor. Someone will have to go inside, and blast a hole for them to shoot through.

Getting inside

Arriving at the thermal oscillator, Finn and his friends find that their path is blocked by a heavy blast door.

Finn and Rey need to find a way to open it. Rey realizes that the Starkiller uses the same technology as the old Imperial ships she scavenged on Jakku.

Rey finds the box controlling the blast door and tears a piece out of it. When the door opens, Han and Chewie rush inside and place their explosives. There is a huge explosion, and a hole appears in the Starkiller's armor. The Resistance's X-wings attack and finish the job. The Resistance has won!

Mission accomplished

The thermal oscillator has been destroyed, and the Starkiller is starting to tear itself apart, but Finn's mission isn't over. Kylo Ren, the First Order's greatest warrior, is coming after Finn and Rey.

Finn battles Kylo Ren using his lightsaber, but Kylo is stronger and better trained. Finn is injured and knocked unconscious.

While he is unconscious, Rey picks up Finn's lightsaber and defeats Kylo. Afterward, she and Finn are taken back to the Resistance base where Finn is treated in the medical center. When he is healed, Finn will rejoin the battle against the First Order.

Quiz

1. What was Finn's stormtrooper name?

2. Which planet was Finn's first battle on?

3. What was the name of the Resistance pilot rescued by Finn?

4. What are the names of the gangs that attack Han and Chewie?

5. Who is the legendary pirate who lives in a castle?

6. Which planet is the Resistance base hidden on?

7. What is the name of the First Order's superweapon?

8. Who is the First Order's greatest warrior?

Answers on page 64

Glossary

Carnivorous
Something that only eats meat

Empire
An evil group that once ruled the galaxy, but which was defeated

First Order
A new army formed by the survivors of the Empire

Force
A strange energy with a light side and a dark side

Freighter
A ship designed to transport cargo

General
Someone who leads soldiers in battle

Impenetrable
Impossible to get through

Lightsaber
A sword that has a glowing laser blade

Omnivorous
Something that eats both meat and plants

Poaching
When someone steals animals from someone else

Rebellion
When someone
tries to free
themselves from
the control of
another

Resistance
A group created
to protect the
galaxy from the
First Order

Scavenger
Someone who
searches through
worthless junk
to try and find
useful things

Starship
A vehicle
used to travel
through space

Guide for Parents

This book is part of an exciting four-level reading series for children, developing the habit of reading widely for both pleasure and information. These chapter books have a compelling main narrative to suit your child's reading ability. Each book is designed to develop your child's reading skills, fluency, grammar awareness, and comprehension in order to build confidence and engagement when reading.

Ready for a *Level 3* book

YOUR CHILD SHOULD

- be able to read many words without needing to stop and break them down into sound parts.

- read smoothly, in phrases and with expression.
  By this level, your child will be beginning to read silently.

- self-correct when a word or sentence doesn't sound right.

A valuable and shared reading experience

For some children, text reading, particularly nonfiction, requires much effort, but adult participation can make this both fun and easier. So here are a few tips on how to use this book with your child.

TIP 1 Check out the contents together before your child begins:

- invite your child to check the back cover text, contents page, and layout of the book and comment on it.

- ask your child to make predictions about the story.

- talk about the information your child might want to find out.

TIP 2 Encourage fluent and flexible reading:

- support your child to read in fluent, expressive phrases, making full use of punctuation and thinking about the meaning.
- help your child learn to read with expression by choosing a sentence to read aloud and demonstrating how to do this.

TIP 3 Indicators that your child is reading for meaning:

- your child will be responding to the text if he/she is self-correcting and varying his/her voice.
- your child will want to talk about what he/she is reading or is eager to turn the page to find out what will happen next.

TIP 4 Chat at the end of each chapter:

- encourage your child to recall specific details after each chapter.
- let your child pick out interesting words and discuss what they mean.
- talk about what each of you found most interesting or most important.
- ask questions about the text. These help to develop comprehension skills and awareness of the language used.

A FEW ADDITIONAL TIPS

- Read to your child regularly to demonstrate fluency, phrasing, and expression; to find out or check information; and for sharing enjoyment.
- Encourage your child to reread favorite texts to increase reading confidence and fluency.
- Check that your child is reading a range of different types of material, such as poems, jokes, and following instructions.

Index

BB-8 28, 30, 48

Chewbacca 34–35, 38–39, 40, 46, 48, 52

Finn 15, 18–19, 20–21, 26–27, 30–31, 32, 34–35, 39, 46, 48–49, 50, 52–53, 54–55, 56–57

First Order 5, 7, 9, 10, 13, 14, 16–17, 26, 30, 32–33, 46–47, 48, 50, 54, 56, 57

Guavian Death Gang 39

Han 34–35, 38–39, 40, 46, 48, 52

Happabore 21, 23

Jakku 8–9, 12, 18, 22, 24, 30, 47

Kanjiklub 39

Kylo Ren 56–57

Leia 48–49

Maz 40, 42–43, 44, 46

Maz's castle 42–43, 44, 46

Millennium Falcon 31, 32–33, 34–35, 39, 52

Niima Outpost 20, 24–25, 26, 28

Poe 15, 18–19, 27, 28, 47

Rathtar 35, 36–37

Resistance 10, 14, 27, 28, 47, 48–49, 53, 55, 57

Rey 26–27, 28, 30, 32–33, 34–35, 47, 53, 54, 56–57

Star Destroyer 14, 16, 18

Starkiller 50–51, 52–53, 56

Stormtroopers 4–5, 9, 10, 12–13, 16, 26–27, 46, 51

TIE fighter 15, 16–17, 18, 30, 32, 51

Answers to the quiz on pages 58 and 59:
1. FN-2187 2. Jakku 3. Poe Dameron 4. Kanjiklub and Guavian Death Gang 5. Maz Kanata
6. D'Qar 7. the Starkiller 8. Kylo Ren